by Dot Meharry
illustrated by Julian Bruère

Harcourt
SCHOOL PUBLISHERS

Printed in China

ISBN 10: 0-15-350635-0
ISBN 13: 978-0-15-350635-2

Ordering Options
ISBN 10: 0-15-350599-0 (Grade 2 On-Level Collection)
ISBN 13: 978-0-15-350599-7 (Grade 2 On-Level Collection)
ISBN 10: 0-15-357808-4 (package of 5)
ISBN 13: 978-0-15-357808-3 (package of 5)

4 5 6 7 8 9 10   985   15 14 13 12 11 10 09 08

One morning, Duck looked at the
pond in the woods. It was covered
with leaves. "I will clean up the pond
for Frog," she said.

Duck swam through the leaves.
She gathered them up in her beak.
She put them in a pile at the edge of
the pond.

4

Then Duck picked up the leaves
and dropped them under the trees
in the woods. "Frog will never guess
who cleaned up the pond," she said
when she had finished.

Duck sat in her nest. "What a
surprise Frog will get," she thought.
"He will be pleased." Soon Duck was
fast asleep.

While Duck slept, the wind blew.
Leaves fell off the trees in the woods
and into the pond.

Frog swam up from the bottom
of the pond. Leaves covered
everything—even the pond. "I will
clean up the pond for Duck," he said.

Frog swam through the leaves.
He gathered them up in his mouth.
He put them in a pile at the edge of
the pond.

Then Frog picked up the leaves
and dropped them under the trees
in the woods. "Duck will never guess
who cleaned up the pond," he said
when he had finished.

Frog sat down on a lily pad.
"What a surprise Duck will get," he
thought. "She will be pleased." Soon
Frog was fast asleep.

Duck and Frog slept for a long
time. The wind blew. Leaves fell
off the trees in the woods and into
the pond.

Duck woke up and saw leaves everywhere. She jumped into the pond and began to gather them up in her beak.

Frog woke up and saw leaves everywhere. He jumped into the pond and began to gather them up in his mouth.

Bump! Duck and Frog bumped into each other. What a surprise they got!

"I can guess what you're doing," mumbled Frog through the leaves in his mouth.

"Let's clean up together," laughed Duck.

Think Critically

1. What happened when the wind blew?

2. How are Duck and Frog alike?

3. Why did Duck and Frog bump into each other?

4. How do you think Duck and Frog felt when they woke up and saw the leaves in the pond again?

5. How did this story make you feel?

 **Social Studies**

Write Sentences Write three sentences about the differences between where you live and where Duck and Frog live.

School-Home Connection Show family members the cover of *Bump!* Ask them what they think the story is about. Then tell them the story and talk about different animals that live in a pond.